BFI FILM CLASSICS

Rob White
SERIES EDITOR

Edward Buscombe, Colin MacCabe and David Meeker
SERIES CONSULTANTS

Cinema is a fragile medium. Many of the great films now exist, if at all, in damaged or incomplete prints. Concerned about the deterioration in the physical state of our film heritage, the National Film and Television Archive, part of the British Film Institute's Collections Department, has compiled a list of 360 key works in the history of the cinema. The long-term goal of the Archive is to build a collection of perfect showprints of these films, which will then be screened regularly at the National Film Theatre in London in a year-round repertory.

BFI Film Classics is a series of books intended to introduce, inter-pret and honour these 360 films. Critics, scholars, novelists and those distinguished in the arts have been invited to write on a film of their choice, drawn from the Archive's list. The numerous illustrations have been made specially from the Archive's own prints.

With new titles published each year, the BFI Film Classics series is a unique, authoritative and highly readable guide to the masterpieces of world cinema.

The best movie publishing idea of the [past] decade.
Philip French, *The Observer*

Exquisitely dimensioned … magnificently concentrated examples of freeform critical poetry.
Uncut

D1210464

BFI FILM CLASSICS

BELLE DE JOUR

. . . .

Michael Wood

bfi Publishing

First published in 2000 by the
BRITISH FILM INSTITUTE
21 Stephen Street, London W1P 2LN

The British Film Institute
promotes greater understanding
and appreciation of, and
access to, film and moving image
culture in the UK.

British Library Cataloguing-in-Publication Data
A catalogue record for this book is available from the British Library

ISBN 0–85170–823–4

Series design by
Andrew Barron & Collis Clements Associates

Typeset in Fournier and Franklin Gothic by
D R Bungay Associates, Burghfield, Berks

Printed in Great Britain by Cromwell Press, Trowbridge, Wiltshire

CONTENTS

. . . .

The camera's gaze

INTRODUCTION
. . . .

'Younger men get older every day,' Richie Havens used to sing with droning and seemingly irrefutable logic. Luis Buñuel too got older as a director, shifting from outright iconoclasm in France and Spain to making a living in the Mexican commercial cinema. But then suddenly he stopped. International success, far from confirming his maturity, simply broke the clock. From *Viridiana* (1961), made when Buñuel was sixty-one, to *That Obscure Object of Desire* (1977), made when he was seventy-seven, there is not the slightest sign of ageing, only a few subtle shifts of tone. After that Buñuel got a little older in body, too frail to make another movie, and then in 1983 he died.

Older men, this career suggests, don't have to get older every day. But they are not immune to history, they have habits and obsessions, and if they are working directors they accumulate films behind them, a form of personal and public memory. Buñuel's weird youthfulness of spirit, and his displaced life, interrupted by the Spanish Civil War, converted into a Mexican exile which was also home, mean we can't draw a map of his career in conventional terms. There is an early Surrealist section, a missing middle, and a miscellaneous, unclassifiable area where the middle might have been. Some great films are dotted throughout a period of more than forty-five years: *Un Chien andalou* (1928), *L'Age d'or* (1930), *Los Olvidados* (1950), *El* (1952), *The Criminal Life of Archibaldo de la Cruz* (1955), *The Exterminating Angel* (1962) and *The Discreet Charm of the Bourgeoisie* (1972). But this career, unorthodox in so many other regards, does have an unmistakable late period, marked by an amazing series of glossy and troubling works shot in colour and (mainly) in France. *Viridiana*, we might say, announces this period but doesn't quite belong to it. Late, in this sense, doesn't mean either magisterial or weary or irresponsible. It means … well, this book tries to show what it means through a close look at a single film, and argues that for the ageless Buñuel, in any event, lateness began with *Belle de Jour*.

1

....

STYLES OF IMPATIENCE

Buñuel liked to insist that he had no film style, or that the best styles are invisible. These are two not entirely compatible claims, but they point in a single direction: style is not to be detachable, a distraction. Starting from his silent Surrealist films and working through his Mexican works Buñuel converted a mixture of invention and indulged ineptness – too much skill or familiarity with film grammar would be close to capitulation to the mainstream – into a fully intentional ragged poise, a careful flouting of rules of composition and sequence. In their later years he and Gabriel Figueroa, director of photography on *Los Olvidados*, *El*, *Nazarín* (1958), *La Fièvre monte à El Pao* (1959), *The Young One* (1960) and *The Exterminating Angel*, would make jokes and tell stories about their old differences. Roughly, Figueroa knew how to get a wonderful, haunting, harmonious look on the screen, and Buñuel took that as the measure of what he didn't want – a standard of beauty he could turn into awkwardness. Of course he also left many of the frames to Figueroa's taste, or made his films out of a combination of their two tastes, so the final result isn't all awkward – just liable to tip into awkwardness when least expected.

In spite of his claims, then, Buñuel's film style is visible to anyone who cares to look, best defined perhaps as a form of impatience, a refusal to wait around for glamour or contemplation. It's the impatience which makes the slow moments stand out – like the shot of the little girl leaving a plague-stricken house in *Nazarín*, trailing a long sheet behind her. Buñuel is not going to linger on his story or his images, but a whole epidemic is in this picture of a bereft, crying child, and Buñuel knows he needs to stay with this shot, and allow its beauty to confirm its desolation. Conversely, moments like this remind us how brusque and even brutal the rest of the visual action is.

Buñuel's discreet efficiency in this respect is more persistent than his occasional filmic gags – the egg thrown at the lens in *Los Olvidados*, the two marginally different takes of the same scene in *The Exterminating Angel* – but not less disconcerting. The effect not only converts a supposed absence of style into a style that is instantly recognisable, it makes the world on the screen look curiously optional and unstable, however

realistically it is set up. Buñuel, the most careful of movie-makers, creates a discreet impression of carelessness not by the speed of his shooting schedule – which is always cited but was not unusual for commercial directors in Mexico or the United States at the time – but by the speed with which he arrives at and leaves whatever scene he is showing. Look at this, the camera says, but look quickly, because it will be gone in a moment. There is nothing here like the exploratory pace of say Visconti, or even Welles or Fellini. What is often thought to be coldness in Buñuel is also an aspect of this speed. He rarely stays long enough with anything to look as if he cares. His care is of another order.

Belle de Jour was not Buñuel's first colour film, but it was his farewell to black-and-white. The director of photography was Sacha Vierny, probably best known for his work with Alain Resnais (*Night and Fog*, 1955, *Hiroshima mon amour*, 1959, *Last Year at Marienbad*, 1961), who has also, more recently, done films for Peter Greenaway (from *A Zed and Two Noughts*, 1985, to *Prospero's Books*, 1991). Vierny didn't work with Buñuel again, and I don't think we can we make a big interpretative deal out of the conjunction of the three just-named directors – except perhaps to wonder

The child and the plague in *Nazarín*

why we think of Resnais and Greenaway as stylists while we see Buñuel as something like the reverse. Vierny, I would suggest, introduces or allows into Buñuel's work an idea of visual style which would otherwise be quite alien to it, and which becomes part of his signature.

The impatience doesn't change, or the speed. But the raggedness, the programmatic awkwardness goes. Is Buñuel now less afraid of beauty? He understands, as I shall suggest later, that beauty may contain its own satire, but only, I would guess he thinks, in colour. Beauty in black-and-white often edges towards starkness, austerity. It can become static, but is not likely to become comic. Beauty in colour easily slides towards the calendar or the coffee-table book, towards tones of mush and self-parody – think of a film like De Sica's *Garden of the Finzi-Continis* (1970). Just the context Buñuel now wants to flirt with, although not exactly to enter. More precisely, Buñuel gets the straight looks of a beautifully photographed world to do a lot of the work that awkwardness used to do for him.

Séverine's Paris

All the old narrative economy remains. No sooner does a person mention an address in *Belle de Jour* than we are looking at the street that's just been named. When a character needs to find out where someone lives we simply see his friend starting to tail the person in question: no following of the following, the character just shows up in the right place, duly instructed between the frames. The Duke in this film, meeting the heroine in an open-air cafe, says he'll give her a lift to his château one day. The camera pans to the right across his horse-drawn carriage and up towards the coachmen, as if mildly pointing to the means of transport, and there's a sudden cut to a shot of the same carriage seen from a quite different angle, coming from the left. The heroine is sitting in it, on her way.

The long-held shot which opens *Belle de Jour* ends as the camera, after letting an old-fashioned carriage approach, go past and continue on ahead, slowly pans up a row of trees toward the sky. Another director would pause here, allow us to absorb the scenery and make sense of the

The landau approaches

The camera takes to the trees

Séverine's coachmen

implied location, particularly after the leisurely, 'aesthetic' timing of the rest of the shot. Buñuel cuts before the tree tops are in view, shows us the carriage coming straight towards us in long shot, and cuts sharply from there to a rather strained frontal close-up of the two coachmen seen from a low angle between the figures of the two jogging horses. The effect is untidy, not because the images are not beautiful, but because their beauty has been bundled up too rapidly. Buñuel won't wait any longer than needed for the story he has to tell, and we are likely to feel, if we feel anything about it at all, that he hasn't waited long enough. We are already identifying, perhaps without knowing it, Buñuel's style: a way of flinging a world at us, like litter, rather than laying it out, like a lawn.

Something of this effect is present even when Buñuel slows the action down, as he notoriously does in the shot of the natty black patent shoes on the staircase leading to the Paris apartment of Mme Anaïs, the place where our troubled heroine is to spend her afternoons and earn her sobriquet as Belle de Jour – the name of a variety of convolvulus, Freddy Buache tells us, although I'm not sure either Buñuel or Joseph Kessel knew that. Séverine, the heroine, has already visited Mme Anaïs and arranged to return, but she's still uncertain about whether she can go through with her plan. The shoes are the form her uncertainty takes on film. The camera waits on the landing below Mme Anaïs's floor. The legs and shoes of a woman come into view, climbing towards us. We see the hem of her black coat and the bottom of her black handbag swinging lightly in the top corner of the frame. Her steps get slower as she comes up the stairs, and on one step she briefly stops completely. She continues to the landing where we are, and we see her shoes, now very close to us, almost execute a full turn, swivelling neatly towards the direction they came from. Then, with an air of timid decision, they swivel back towards the next flight of stairs. All this in a single shot, which persists as the legs and shoes climb the steps beyond the landing. The next shot is a close-up of the doorbell of Mme Anaïs's apartment. A gloved hand rings the bell.

The camera is relatively patient here, but it knows where to wait, and Buñuel has of course decided on the shoes rather than any other piece of the person or her attire. By this stage – after *Viridiana* and *Diary of a Chambermaid* (1964) – shoes were an expected part of Buñuel's signature on film, not so much a fetish as a joke. There is a delicacy in his staying away from Deneuve's face at this difficult moment, a form of directorly tact, as if the moment were too embarrassing for snooping. But of course there also is the delightful suggestion that these neat little shoes are on their way to misbehave, that a fastidious fashion is about to get itself involved in sleaze. And indeed, a little later, when she is stripped down to bra and pants and being mauled by her first client, Séverine is still wearing the little shoes – a modern Cinderella at the brothel ball. In showing us these shoes on the stairs, as with the abandoned trees at the beginning, Buñuel is working in a kind of shorthand, leaving inferences to us, where another director, most directors perhaps, would have treated us to a considered picture of the state of Séverine's soul. Imagine Bergman, for instance, showing us shoes instead of faces. The analogy here would be with the two pairs of shoes and legs arriving at a station in Hitchcock's *Strangers on a Train* (1951), boarding a carriage, and finally meeting in a

Travelling feet in *Strangers on a Train*

compartment, where we are allowed to see the rest of Robert Young and Farley Grainger. Séverine's approach to the brothel is more like a scene in a murder mystery than like an episode in any realistic psychology. Although of course Buñuel's tone is different again from Hitchcock's, even if both have a touch of comedy: doubts are not the same as suspense.

This shot also points to another crucial feature of Buñuel's style. He isn't patient, but he likes his camera to be waiting for his characters. Characteristically he picks them up in the shot, and stays with them until a particular action is completed. He doesn't cut during the action, and he often cuts, with or without transitions, to another self-contained shot which is a scene. A Paris taxi comes round a corner from the left, stops. Deneuve gets out on the side facing us, says goodbye to someone inside.

The taxi drives off. Deneuve crosses the road, walking away from us. As she approaches her apartment building, the camera leaves her, pans calmly up the façade to the second floor. Again all in a single shot. Buñuel is saying: This is where this character lives (and in small part, how she lives). But he could have done it in a series of cuts, as many directors would have. Again, when Séverine, in one of her fantasies, is dragged out of a carriage and whipped, the camera waits to one side, pans up to look at the coachmen, then pans back to pick up Séverine. The coachmen now enter the frame and take her off, and the camera follows them some way into the bushes before the next cut. Or again, in what is no doubt the most elaborate set-up in *Belle de Jour*, the camera waits on the landing of an office building for a lift to arrive at that floor. Two men – from the antecedent action we know they have just robbed a bank messenger – come out of the lift, and walk towards us, then march off down the stairs to the right, a slight movement of the camera allowing us to follow them. We briefly lose sight of them but stay where we are. Looking down through a fancy wrought iron banister we see the next landing, where the stairs divide, and the men now come into the

Who shall escape whipping?

Art Nouveau robbery

frame and pause there, visually caught in the curves of the iron grille. Then they separate, each down a different half of the staircase.

Buñuel much admired the work of Carl Theodor Dreyer – he wrote in an early article of the 'sorrowful geography' of the faces in *The Passion of Joan of Arc* (1927) – but we can't conscript him for the school of those film-makers who, according to André Bazin, 'put their faith in reality' as distinct from 'the image'. Buñuel is not much of a one for depth of field either, although there is one striking scene in *Belle de Jour* which is constructed exactly along the lines Bazin liked to analyse in the work of Orson Welles and William Wyler. At the brothel, two people, Mme Anaïs and Henri Husson, are in the front of the frame, two more, the women who work there, are in the middle ground, and right at the back, her face turned away from us, is Séverine, the subject of the others' conversation and the chief object of our attention, particularly at this moment: her dramatic importance is in inverse proportion to her distance from us. There isn't a lot of this, though, and at a crucial moment in *Belle de Jour*, when it might seem that he would want the faces of both his heroine and her unfortunate husband in focus, Buñuel concentrates on hers, leaving his blurry. The technique is to point, rather than to hover and explore.

Buñuel doesn't 'chop the world up into little fragments', which is Bazin's derogatory definition of montage (as I shall suggest later, when Buñuel does use meaningful juxtapositions in the manner of Eisenstein, he is joking). But he doesn't unroll whole areas of world either, the way Renoir or Visconti does. He has no conviction that film can show us things as they are or that things as they are are worth showing. Buñuel's camera is not a prowler or a neutral observer, it behaves like someone who has

15

Bergman's *Persona*

'We are as close to her as we shall ever be'

been tipped off. It is like a spy with good informants; a spy in a hurry. It waits for the action, shows us what there is, and moves on.

This is true even of the sequences towards the end of *Belle de Jour*, which are as subtle and precise as anything Buñuel ever shot. Here something like exploration is taking place, a whole tender tour of Séverine's imagined feelings – that is, the feelings we impute to her as Buñuel allows us to scrutinise, at length, her face and her gestures. We might almost be in a Bergman movie here, *Persona* (1966) say. Séverine moves around her apartment like a person who thinks everything in sight is breakable, including the people. We are as close to her as we shall ever be. But then Buñuel turns out to have another trick up his sleeve. This isn't a Bergman actress, it's Catherine Deneuve. She's good, but she specialises in distance rather than depth. Buñuel's brush with psychology is over. He tilts us back into mystery, leaves us staring at a world we thought, for a second, we were going to understand.

2

....

PRODUCTION VALUES

After *Belle de Jour*, Serge Silberman was the producer of all of Buñuel's films except *Tristana* (1970), which was backed by a consortium of companies in Spain. Silberman was an energetic and intelligent admirer of Buñuel's work, and their collaboration, if not always quiet, was of the happiest. Buñuel had no such relations with Robert and Raymond Hakim, the producers of *Belle de Jour*, who approached him with a proposal for a film based on the novel by Joseph Kessel, and starring Catherine Deneuve. But the place of the Hakim brothers in film history is not negligible. They were in the business a long time, and produced Jean Renoir's *La Bête humaine* (1938) as well as René Clément's marvellous *Plein Soleil* (1960), recently remade as *The Talented Mr Ripley* (1999). They persuaded Buñuel to take out of the film the more luridly blasphemous section of a scene of necrophilia, a cut which he later called 'stupid', but they don't seem otherwise to have interfered, and they did give Buñuel a taste for film-making luxury, or at least ease, which he never abandoned. One of the names for the supposed mellowness of Buñuel's late films is money.

And of course Catherine Deneuve was a fabulous gift to Buñuel – one he recognised and reciprocated by casting her again in *Tristana*. She had made some sixteen films by the time she came to *Belle de Jour*, but was best known for two highly contrasting roles: the doll-like innocent in Jacques Demy's *Umbrellas of Cherbourg* (1964), and the beleaguered

Dreaming in *The Umbrellas of Cherbourg*

hysteric in Roman Polanski's *Repulsion* (1965). Raymond Durgnat says Deneuve's Séverine is 'halfway between the heroines' of these two films, but perhaps Buñuel is rather suggesting that the second of these characters could be hiding in the first – hiding so well that we can only guess she's there. Durgnat observes that Deneuve 'beautifully catches the vague sullenness' of the character she plays: 'her beautiful eyes glaze over, suddenly clicking back to reality, disappointedly; her jaw becomes mournfully slack, giving her face a skull-like quality under its soft whiteness.' Carlos Fuentes remarks that in *Belle de Jour* she 'is constantly looking outside the confines of the screen'. Buñuel himself said that when he first met her she was 'very beautiful, reserved, and strange' (*'muy bella, reservada y extraña'*).

Deneuve brings to all her early roles – her recent work, say in *Indochine* (1991) or *Le Temps retrouvé* (1999), is rather different – an extraordinary capacity for seeming not to be there. Her face in *Belle de Jour* is pale, pure, often startled, sometimes harsh, usually empty: the face of a lovely clown, or a sleepwalker. The dark eyes and lashes, in the white face, under the fair hair, create a slightly eerie impression, as if she was more than one person. When she is supposed to drop a vase full of flowers by accident, she can't do it: she manifestly throws the thing on the floor. Poor acting, this, probably – or it would have been had Buñuel not chosen to keep the shot. As it is, it looks as if the character is pretending to drop the vase, trying to control the very realm of chance, as if she thinks nervousness itself is a matter of icy discipline, to be satisfied by a fastidious imitation of the distress you really feel. Deneuve repeatedly says she's sorry in *Belle de Jour* but she never once looks sorry. The strong implication is that her character knows how she ought to feel but actually feels something else: impatient, perhaps.

Deneuve's clothes and hairdos, of course, as has often been said, add hugely to the sense of someone who is meant to be looked at but can't be understood – either because her privacy is so securely locked away inside her or because there is no one there to be understood. Buñuel gets Yves Saint-Laurent to dress her in neat, shortish suits and dresses and coats, all with a slightly military air, as if she were a fabulous, feminine, frosty toy soldier. In the last scene in the film she wears a sober little black dress with a large white collar. Michel Piccoli, as Henri Husson, visits her apartment and comments on her dress. Pretty, he says. 'You look like a precocious schoolgirl' ('*On dirait une collégienne précoce*'). Deneuve's first film, released in 1957, was called *Les Collégiennes*. There is some resemblance here to what Hitchcock does with his blondes from Grace Kelly to Kim Novak to Tippi Hedren, where the woman, in each case, becomes a doll to be dressed up and manipulated, even violated, by the director and by the chief male character. But Deneuve is not a doll in *Belle de Jour*, she is an enigma.

Among the first and last words of the film is the question of what she is thinking about, and although the question is answered each time – she is thinking of an old-fashioned carriage and coachmen, with various fantasies to follow – it outlasts the answer, continues to make its little ripples of mystery. We can't know what she is thinking, even when we have ostensibly seen a picture of it, and this is unmistakably Deneuve's contribution to the movie: an air of secrecy, a remoteness from whatever is going on, which almost recalls that of Marlene Dietrich in her films with Joseph von Sternberg. The same is true of a central image in the film where Deneuve doesn't look icy or sullen but supremely relaxed and happy. Her character, Séverine, working at a brothel, has just slept with a vast Asian who scares everyone else. The client has gone, and she is lying on the bed face down, hair loose and ruffled. Pallas, the maid at the brothel, expresses her sympathy. 'Me too, I'd be afraid of that man. It must be hard at times, all the same.' The camera closes in on Deneuve, who slowly lifts her head, and whose face expresses fatigue but also a wonderful, weary, deep delight. 'What do you know about it, Pallas?' she says. This is not poor but excellent acting, yet the effect of distance, curiously, remains. Deneuve is as alone with her happiness as she is with anything else. We can read her face, that is, but we are as far as ever from being able to read her mind.

We have to be careful here, though. Deneuve is not a sphinx, an emblem of the eternal mystery of womankind, and we should look at her performance in relation to the work of the other actors in the film, notably Michel Piccoli and Geneviève Page. Deneuve and Piccoli had already worked together in Agnes Varda's wonderfully creepy *Les Créatures* (1966) and Jacques Demy's musical *Les Demoiselles de Rochefort* (1967); Piccoli had already appeared in two Buñuel films (*Evil Eden*, 1956, and *Diary of a Chambermaid*) and was to appear in three more (*The Milky Way*, 1968, *The Discreet Charm of the Bourgeoisie*, *The Phantom of Liberty*, 1974). He is a suave, intelligent and versatile actor who can do all kinds of things, but his dominant screen identity at the time of *Belle de Jour* was that of the intricately defeated characters he played in Jean-Luc Godard's *Contempt* (1963), and in *Diary of a Chambermaid*. There are echoes of unhappiness and self-torture in the performance he gives as Henri Husson, but they are subordinate to an extraordinary, ironic self-possession, and a stylish cruelty which is so suave you could almost mistake it for charm. Nearly the first thing he says to the woman he is with when we meet him is to compliment her on her scars – has she attempted suicide? – and soon after he is making an elegant little speech on his affection for the poor and the working classes. 'I think of them above all when it's snowing. No furcoats, no hope, nothing.' When Pierre amiably says Husson is amusing, Séverine says he is strange, and Husson's friend says he is worse than that. Piccoli brings a weird good humour to the role of this sinister character – as indeed he does to that of the Marquis de Sade in *The Milky Way*. You want to like him although you know you can't, and Buñuel relies on Piccoli's presence to carry an important, largely unstated mood throughout the film: the discreet allure of the thoroughly fallen, those who enjoy the sight of social traps because they have escaped them,

Henri Husson as the voice of temptation

who are free from the hypocrisies of compassion and the clutches of desire. And who are not simply boy-scouts like Pierre – the image is Husson's. 'I used to like them,' Husson says a little later, speaking of Paris brothels. 'A very special perfume, totally subservient women ...'. This is not pleasant, but uttered by anyone other than Piccoli, with his easy, worldly smile, the remark would be merely repellent. Here it captivates Séverine, even as she resists its implications; and half-captivates us, not because the life of the brothel tempts us but because the fellow seems so enviably at home in the skin of the bad guy.

Geneviève Page is another story. She had appeared in *El Cid* (1961), and her memorable, enchanting performance in Billy Wilder's *The Private Life of Sherlock Holmes* (1970) was still to come. In *Belle de Jour*, as the madame of Séverine's brothel, she manages, miraculously, to convey an air of sleaze – drawl, cigarette in mouth, tough language – while seeming to deny the very thought that sleaze could exist. This is not just a professional trick, a matter of the assumed social graces inherent in the career her character has chosen within the film. She is not just playing

Mme Anaïs as the averted face of vice

Mme Anaïs gets tough

Husson and Séverine at the brothel

'More than usual affection'

the hostess. She is quietly displaying her independence of mind and taste, so that while we think she knows the world and has probably had her sorrows, neither we nor her clients will ever confuse her with one of the girls who work for her. Her delicate touches of more than usual affection for Belle de Jour – she kisses her on the lips, thoughtfully toasts her in person when the others are just lifting their glasses in general jollity, is hurt when Séverine says she can't come back and won't leave any kind of address or means of staying in contact – suggest both tenderness and difference, a private life well separated from her public appearances. Above all, Page manages to remain cool without seeming chilly, and although she is never ruffled, no one would mistake her for a toy soldier.

Deneuve, Piccoli and Page, then, all convey stories which are a little larger, more interesting or more peculiar than their literal roles in the movie. In part, this is just to say they are actors, that their job, beautifully done, is to have made the script something more than a script. But there is something else, something that makes them prime collaborators of Buñuel in this film. Deneuve's apparent absence, Piccoli's criss-crossing charm and cruelty, Page's implied private life, all help to build one of *Belle de Jour*'s principal implied arguments about the world. It's not that we all have secrets, although we probably do. It's that there is always another story. Whole new or denied territories of fear and desire will open up if we take another turn in the road – if we took the turn we just passed, for example. Actors, if they are lucky, work in other films or plays as well as the one we're seeing, they have other jobs, and other existences beyond those jobs. And most people, Buñuel would say, actors or not, have other, scarier or more delightful lives quite apart from the one they firmly imagine to be their own.

3

....

BUÑUEL AND THE NOVEL

The time-frame is a little uncertain at the start. We see the long drive of what appears to be a private park, or the grounds of a country house. We are inside the grounds, looking down from some height. We glimpse, right at the back of the shot, the gates of the domain, the remote boundary of the public world outside. Is there anything else in sight? There is an open carriage, drawn by two horses, but we hardly see it at first. It comes towards us steadily, we get a clearer view, and we begin to hear the sound of the bells of the horses' harness. This jingling sound is then crossed or overlaid by the long sound of a horn, perhaps coming from a train or a river boat. The second is slightly more likely, since we seem to see water through the trees to the left. There is something intrusive about the sound of the horn, as if another world, more modern or more commercial, insisted on haunting, however discreetly, the carriage and the park. The carriage is driven by a coachman in livery, and another fellow, similarly attired, sits beside him, his arms crossed. A period movie, then. End of the 19th century, perhaps. No, because as the carriage gets closer, we see the passengers, a man and a woman, and they are smartly dressed in 60s suits – by Yves Saint-Laurent, as it happens, at least in the case of the woman's nifty red number.

The screenplay, in an opening scene which was not filmed, has an explanation for this overlap in time. The young man in the carriage has hired the old-time carriage and drivers as an anniversary present for his wife. She is a little surprised, and says, 'What a strange idea.' He says, already revealing something of the literalism of his imagination, 'I've often heard you say that your dream was to ride in a landau.' They pick up the carriage in the Bois de Boulogne, and if we follow this particular spatial and narrative logic, what we took for a park becomes an empty avenue in the Bois. The couple are playing at living in the past, although we very soon learn that the wife's dreams don't stop at going for a ride in a landau.

Within the completed film, we are given another reading of this carriage and this park, also summoned by nostalgia. Both belong to a gaunt and handsome Duke, who picks up the young wife in a cafe in the Bois de Boulogne, in a scene where Buñuel himself, as if to complicate the fictional framework a little further, is sitting at another table. The Duke remarks that he is a man of another age, although as with the wife's dreams of riding in a landau, he turns out to mean rather more than he seems to say. 'An age', he says, 'when one still had a feeling for death.' His feeling for death, as far as we can tell, involves masturbating under a coffin which contains a sequence of virtually nude young women impersonating his dead daughter. It's good to keep in touch with the family. As a matter of filmic fact, the screenplay tells us that the drive we see at the beginning of the finished movie is the drive of the domain which later serves as the Duke's château, wherever we choose to situate the drive in story space.

There is yet another source for the *fin de siècle* look of the opening, its only source in the strictest sense. It comes not from Joseph Kessel's novel, which was written and set in the 20s, but from Buñuel's early imaginings of a film he was to make later, *That Obscure Object of Desire*. 'That idea', he told José de la Colina and Tomás Pérez Turrent, 'really comes from *La Femme et le pantin*, from the first time I thought of filming it'. *La Femme et le pantin*, literally *The Woman and the Puppet*, or *The Woman and the Marionette*, an 1898 novel by Pierre Louÿs, had already been filmed by Joseph von Sternberg (with Marlene Dietrich) as *The Devil is a Woman* (1935), and by Julien Duvivies (with Brigitte Bardot) as *La Femme et le pantin* (1969). But of course Buñuel's 'idea' wasn't just the park and the landau. Like the young wife and the Duke, he has a whole sequence in mind. 'It's that the image of two *fin de siècle* lackeys, with top hats, insignia, and gold buttons on their tunics, whipping a naked woman, seems interesting to me.' More precisely, since Buñuel lends this image to the woman herself, it is interesting to him and to her, to director and character, and for this reason interesting to us as an intricately borrowed and lent fantasy.

What happens in the film is this. In a second shot the carriage comes towards us, rolling through an avenue of faintly autumnal trees and fallen leaves. There is a close-up of the horses' heads, and we see the burly, impassive coachmen between them. We pick up the young couple in medium close-up, and we hear their soppy dialogue, and learn their names. 'Would you like me to tell you a secret, Séverine?' the young man says. 'I love you more every day.' 'Me too, Pierre,' Séverine says. 'You're all I have in the world.' There's something wrong with this idyll, though. Pierre says he would like everything to be perfect, would like Séverine's 'coldness' to disappear. She says angrily that he is not to talk of that, and he rather mawkishly says he has 'an immense tenderness' for her. She snaps, '*A quoi peut-elle me servir, ta tendresse?*' ('What good is your tenderness to me?'). Pierre drops back in his seat, remarking on how unkind she can be, and she says she is sorry.

At this point Pierre's attitude changes entirely. He stops the carriage, orders Séverine to get out, starts to drag her from her seat, gets the coachmen to help him. They haul her off through the forest, gag her and tie her up, joining Pierre in shouting insults at her. Pierre tears off the back of her dress and her bra, and the two coachmen, from some distance, lash her with their long horsewhips. After a while Pierre says that's enough, and hands her over to the coachmen. One of them, the rather more brutal-looking of the two, takes off his coat and hat, puts his hands on Séverine and kisses her back. We know what comes next. Her face in close-up expresses, according to the French screenplay, 'a mixture of fear and expectation', according to the English version, 'a mixture of repugnance and pleasure'. I'm not sure I know what her face expresses. In any event, she throws her head back, and closes her eyes.

Certain elements in this sequence have already indicated that we are in a fantasy or a Buñuel film, or both. There are the cats Séverine suddenly mentions in the middle of her whipping. 'Pierre, I beg of you, don't let the cats loose.' What cats? There is the comic behaviour of the coachman who can't quite get the syntax of respect out of his attempt at insult: 'Shut up, madam, or I'll smash your face in.' And there is the broken logic of the whole scene, the abrupt and dreamlike conversion of tenderness into violence, as if to illustrate the secret cohabitation of opposites. In any case, we are not long left in doubt. We hear Pierre's voice over Séverine's face with closed eyes, and he is saying, in a tone much closer to that of his first remarks, 'What are you thinking about, Séverine?' We see Pierre coming out of a posh 60s bathroom, buttoning up his immaculate pyjamas, and he repeats his question. Séverine is in bed. She says, 'I was thinking about you. … About us. We were riding together in a landau.' Pierre smiles, and says, '*Toujours le landau?*' ('That landau again?'). Now we know where we are. The time is the present and the place is a bedroom. The carriage is neither hired for an anniversary, nor borrowed from a Duke, nor even, within the fiction, part of the repertory of obsessive images of a Spanish film-maker. It is the moving furniture of Séverine's recurring daydream, familiar enough to both of

Séverine dreams of violence and submission

'The time is the present and the place is a bedroom'

them, invoked and narrated often enough in this marriage, for Pierre to smile at its reappearance.

But wait a minute. Does she really tell him the whole fantasy? Has she ever told it to him? Realistically, she must have just said she dreams of riding in a carriage, or that they ride in a carriage in her dreams. But for a moment we are faced with one of those startling gaps or lapses so frequent in Buñuel – as where Mathieu, in *That Obscure Object of Desire*, tells his steamy, sexual story to a group of travelling companions on a train, and then is astonished at the thought that he might have said anything unsuitable for children to hear. What if Séverine told Pierre the fantasy exactly as we have seen it, and he's still smiling benignly? Oh, you mean the one where I suddenly turn authoritarian, the one with the masochism and flagellation and rough trade stuff? Was it with or without the cats? Good night, dear. Don't forget we're going skiing tomorrow.

Séverine's daydreams are Buñuel's contribution to the plot-line offered him by Kessel's novel. Indeed Buñuel said that the idea of the two levels of reality, where in Kessel there was only one, was what provoked him to film the story in the first place. Generally, he thought the book was '*un poco folletinesca*', too much like a *feuilleton*, an old-fashioned, sentimental serial novel, and on one occasion he said he didn't like it at all. This was a way of distancing himself from his real debt, perhaps, since the novel already contains a good deal of what he turned out to need. It is shrewd and intelligent throughout, warmly sympathetic to its troubled heroine, only a touch too dedicated, in the end, to the idea of sexuality as a horrible fate and to a melodramatic plotting which guarantees a violent and unhappy end. Kessel's Séverine has thoughts galore, which are delicately analysed for us, but she doesn't have fantasies which displace her in time or break the narrative continuity of her story, let alone make us wonder which of her worlds is real. She has a double life, so to speak, but only one world, in which doubleness itself must at last lead to calamity.

In the novel, Séverine's problem is simple and terminal, resting on what Kessel rather luridly calls, in a preface, 'the terrible divorce between the heart and the flesh, between a true, immense and tender love and the implacable demands of the senses'. She loves Pierre but cannot experience sexual pleasure with him, indeed cannot associate pleasure in any way with marriage, respectability, affection or consent. A brief prologue, describing her molestation by a plumber when she is eight years old – 'The man left her on the wooden floor, went off without a noise. Her governess found Séverine lying there. They believed she had slipped. This is what she believed too' – suggests a traumatic origin for her condition. In the present time of the novel, she is awakened by an illness to a sense of her own body, a feeling abetted by a mild (and unsuccessful) pass made at her by Henri Husson, a friend of a friend of hers. 'You're not the right type for a rapist,' she says. '*Vous n'êtes pas fait pour le viol.*' This sounds as if it ought to be a compliment of sorts, a recognition that a gent is still a gent even when he's a prowler, and Séverine probably means it that way. The novel soon teaches us, though, that rape, for Séverine, cannot come from a member of her own class, and that what she seeks is not rape, since she runs to it so willingly, but something like the social aura of rape, not forced sex but sex as irresistible

Portrait of Séverine as a young victim

social transgression. To say that a middle-class seducer is not a rapist is the same thing as saying her husband is too nice.

Séverine learns that an acquaintance, Henriette, a seemingly well-to-do woman, regularly works in a brothel. Not well-to-do enough, apparently, as she is said to be doing it for the money. Séverine's imagination is transfixed, and after asking both Pierre and Husson what they know about these places, finds her way to the establishment of one Mme Anaïs. But what clinches her decision to work there is the sight of naked desire for her on the face of a bargeman she sees in the street: the brothel is the place where he can have what he wants, and where she can be what he wants and nothing else. She gives him the address, and some money, in case he's broke. He doesn't seem to understand, and has to take off downriver with his barge anyway. He doesn't show up at the brothel, but Séverine does, and her new life is established. She works from two to five, and takes Belle de Jour as her professional name.

It's a hard, dull life, though, and Séverine doesn't find the pleasure she is seeking. The clients are vulgar and undemanding, and what she is after, it seems, is more than sex and social disgrace, and the thrill of misbehaviour. It's true that she gets shivers of pleasure from being pushed around, both by Mme Anaïs and a client – this is said to be an invasion of a 'pride' no one had touched, as if pride could secretly long for its own abasement, as if pride and masochism were a pair. What Séverine enjoys, we are told, is her 'obedience' – the implication is that her married life represents an excessive, enervating freedom, an unwanted, inviolate autonomy. Kessel is using a language of morality for what must be a psychological condition, but the condition itself is clear enough. Séverine experiences a 'horrible delight' ('*une volupté affreuse*') in her humiliation, but still no pleasure in the sexual act itself. When even the delight in humiliation begins to fade, she gets a small kick from thinking about the money paid for her services, and shows a mild experimental interest in the lesbian activities of the other women in the brothel. Until one day a hefty new client appears, and the miracle occurs.

He's drunk, a porter from Les Halles, and Mme Anaïs and the other women are not pleased to see him. He chooses Séverine, possesses her brutally, in silence. His 'coarse fury', his 'bestial lust' frighten and surprise her, but they also do something else. Her face takes on 'such an expression of peace, happiness and youth that anyone other than the man whose prey she had been would have been overwhelmed'. Kessel now

Séverine and Marcel

really goes to town on Séverine's new experience. It's the end of a 'hitherto meaningless martyrdom', it's the acquisition of 'a property no one else has the right to look at'. It's a 'sensual revelation', a 'marvellous bolt of lightning', and most surprisingly perhaps, 'her spiritual joy was greater even than the physical joy which had shaken her with a flux like no other.' Hard to see where Kessel can go after this hymn to liberation, and the novel does get slightly lost here.

Without ceasing for a moment to love her husband in the most elevated and idealised way, Séverine falls in love with Marcel, a young thug who visits the brothel. She likes him as an individual as well as for his louche and dangerous life – his body is covered in scars, a whole history of Parisian knife fights – and the story slips away from the (possibly too threatening) conflict between intimacy without sexual pleasure and sexual pleasure without any care for the person, as long as he is a member of a class that can be seen as brutal and inferior. No longer a matter of the 'implacable demands of the senses' and the 'terrible divorce' between the flesh and the heart, the story now concerns the more familiar, more conventional figure of the rich woman who gets her kicks from slumming, who needs to supplement the boredom of bourgeois life with the spice of forbidden fruit. It's true that Kessel still writes of the 'fear which formed the deepest part of her pleasure', but Séverine's very fear seems shallower now. Once driven by a desperate, half-conscious search for a sexual bliss she had not known, intuitively understanding that only in violence, abasement and anonymity could she even hope to find fulfilment, Séverine now seems to have lost her very appetite for sexual joy, to have displaced it on to its trimmings. The sequence here is very creepy. At first Séverine experiences with Marcel the sort of overwhelming delight she felt with the porter from Les Halles. But when she gets interested in Marcel as an individual the sexual pleasure pales, and she has to resort to urban folklore, to looking for bangs by accompanying him on the side-adventures of his criminal career. A sexual pleasure inflected by social implications has become a social search for pleasure.

Still, this story is more manageable than the other one, and Kessel smoothly sets the machinery of his plot to the task of reaching a conclusion. Séverine's double life collapses twice: once when Marcel learns her real name and address; once when Henri Husson turns up at the brothel and finds her working there. He has no intention of telling

Séverine's dream and Séverine dreaming

Hesitations

Prayers and persecutions. Middle: Jean-François Millet, *The Angelus*
(1857–59), Musée d'Orsay, Paris/The Bridgeman Art Library

Trial and error in the brothel

Séverine meets the Duke (and Buñuel), and Husson pays a visit

Intimacy: Séverine dreams of Husson, is trailed by Hippolyte, and wakes up to the sound of shooting

Time passes and Séverine agonises

Séverine agonises and the world changes behind her

Pierre about Séverine's extra-curricular activities, but he enjoys the sight and the thought of her disarray, and he doesn't tell her that he's not going to tell. Petrified at the thought of Pierre's finding out what she's been doing, Séverine asks Marcel to bump off Husson at the very moment when, she thinks, he is about to spill the beans. Pierre sees Marcel before Husson does, gets in the way, and is stabbed in the temple, incapacitated for life. Marcel goes to jail, but keeps mum, like the stalwart, passionate outlaw that he is. His gangster friend makes sure that Séverine's maid doesn't tell the law what she knows, and everything seems to be sorted out, except for the unfortunate Pierre's medical condition. Husson and Séverine, in a very atmospheric scene, lucidly acknowledge their shared guilt in what has happened, but seem ready to go back to ordinary, conscienceless life the next day. Then Séverine realises that the crippled Pierre, who can't move and who can scarcely talk, is ashamed of his dependence, asking her forgiveness for the trouble he is causing her. Unable to bear the thought of such perfect confidence in her, Séverine tells Pierre everything. Kessel has a fine, open-ended, only slightly over-written paragraph here:

> How to explain such a gesture? By the simple impossibility of displaying a painted virtue to the person she loved infinitely? By the – less noble – need to confess? By the underground hope of being forgiven in spite of everything and of living together thereafter without the burden of a horrible secret? Who could count the elements which, after such frightful passages, are active and combine in a human heart, and put its plight on to trembling lips?

But then Kessel finishes his book on a grim but persuasive absence of pardon. Three years go by. Pierre and Séverine live quietly together by the sea. The last sentence of the novel is: 'But since Séverine spoke, she has not heard Pierre's voice again.'

Buñuel notoriously changed the ending of this story – or more precisely both changed and kept part of it. But it's worth recalling just how much of Kessel's novel he and his co-writer Jean-Claude Carrière retained elsewhere. Husson, Henriette, Anaïs, Marcel, much of the novel's dialogue, some of the customers in the brothel, Séverine's dreamy sexual fulfilment through a client who puts the other women off, Husson's arrival chez Anaïs, Marcel's discovery of Séverine's name and whereabouts, the whole recurring sense of sexuality tangled in social rank – all this is in the film. The film adds a kinky client to the brothel, and turns the porter from Les Halles into a vast Asian, who jingles little bells before he and Séverine get down to it, and who carries a mysterious box from which a persistent humming sound emerges. Buñuel used to say that the only thing anyone wanted to know about any of his works was what was in that box. His answer was invariably, 'How should I know?' The film adds Séverine's daydreams too, the sequence with the Duke and his coffin, which may or may not be a daydream, and very firmly subtracts Kessel's notions of doom and destiny, of what he calls an 'interior fatality' and 'the enemy installed inside her'.

Kessel's weakest claim, in his preface, is his high-minded denial not of Séverine's dilemma but of her momentary freedom. 'The subject of *Belle de Jour* is not Séverine's sensual aberration, it is her love for Pierre which is independent of this aberration.' Buñuel will have none of this. His Séverine courts a masochism of a very special kind: not a pleasure in pain or suffering, but a need to be forced into pleasure. The horror, and temptation, of the brothel, in Kessel, is the indiscriminacy of the sex. 'At the mercy of anyone, however ugly, dirty. To do what he wants, everything he wants.' Buñuel repeats this idea ('You take whoever comes: old or not, lousy-looking or not'), but also refines it to emphasise the abandonment of the will: 'You don't have any choice' ('*on n'a pas le choix*'). Séverine's release from her sexual paralysis, however rough and shabby the means of its achievement, is not an aberration for Buñuel. Or if it is, then her abstracted, dutiful love for Pierre is an aberration too, and probably a worse one. But Buñuel is more likely to be suggesting that there are no aberrations, only human beings trying to find their way through the deceptions and denials of their own desire. His characters are free in the end not because they escape an interior or exterior fatality but because the very idea of destiny is mocked at every turn of their story, and begins to look like the fantasy of moralists who can't face the random surprises of the world or the heart.

Buñuel's temporal shifts, his moving to the 60s of a novel set and written in the 20s, while his 60s heroine dreams of a vaguely pornographic end of the nineteenth century, are meant to disconcert us, of course, to turn time itself into an erratic disorder. But the *fin de siècle* carriage and lackeys are important in another sense. They link, as we have seen, the actual film *Belle de Jour* with the not-yet-actual film *That*

Obscure Object of Desire, thereby connecting two French novels, by Kessel and Louÿs, which concern lost or all-too-found women, and we may think of a third novel about a beleaguered woman, also dating from the *fin de siècle*, in fact literally dated 1900: Octave Mirbeau's *Diary of a Chambermaid*, which Buñuel filmed in 1963, before turning, after an excursion into *Simon of the Desert*, to *Belle de Jour*. We can also recall, if we are willing to add to this calendric confusion, that Buñuel shifted the setting of the Mirbeau novel to 1928 – the year of the publication of *Belle de Jour*, although there is no indication at this stage of an interest in Kessel on Buñuel's part. What he did in *Diary of a Chambermaid* was to convert 1900 not into the present time of the film's production but into a moment of his own past, the years of *Un Chien andalou* and *L'Age d'or*, and the battles surrounding them. If Séverine dreams of the turn of the century, Buñuel could also make the turn of the century dream of Surrealism and the rise of fascism. I don't want to overstress these casual connections, but there is a suggestion here that doesn't seem to me casual.

Buñuel made quite a few films based on novels – '*d'après*', as his credits usually say, '*inspiré par*' or '*basado en*'. The novels include Maupassant's *Pierre et Jean*, Defoe's *Robinson Crusoe*, Brontë's *Wuthering Heights*, Usigli's *Essay in Crime*, Peter Mathiessen's *Travelin' Man*, Galdós' *Nazarín* and *Tristana*, and a number of lesser known works. But the novels by Mirbeau, Kessel and Louÿs form a kind of soft-porn trilogy – or at least they do once Buñuel has made films of them. They come to represent a certain idea of 'France' as a place of elegance, corruption, class-consciousness, repression and insidiously violent desire. Or France itself, on film, comes to represent those things in a kind of social shorthand, and the idea of the end of the nineteenth century, perceived as a dream of luxury and decadence, tops off the idea of France. Buñuel's Spanish films, like *Viridiana* and *Tristana*, are quite different in tone. No one uses the adjectives 'Lubitschian' (Raymond Durgnat) or 'Ophulsian' (Andrew Sarris) about them as they do about *Belle de Jour*. I have my doubts about the appropriateness of the adjectives even here, but they certainly catch something of the delicately comic, discreetly erotic world Buñuel is creating in these French films.

It is the world of Freud in a peculiar sense, if we see Freud as the master of desire and its deceptions. Not just a world interpreted in the light of Freud's thought, although it is that in part, and not just a world where Freud and his school would make a fortune, but a world which is waiting for a Freud who can't, come. This is a Paris which can't become Vienna, London or New York, or even Paris as later generations know it, because it can't leave its own aura as capital city of a confused sexual splendour. This is an end of a century which will never end, because desire is always at home here, intricate, elusive and enchanting, beyond all cure and all condemnation.

4

....

THE INTERPRETATION OF DREAMS

'I don't like psychology,' Buñuel says in *My Last Sigh*, although 'it goes without saying that reading Freud and the discovery of the unconscious meant a lot to me in my youth.' What does it mean to remember Freud and not like psychology? One answer would be that it means making *Belle de Jour*.

'In the end,' Buñuel said of this film, 'the real and the imaginary dissolve into each other. I myself couldn't say what is real and what is imaginary in the film. For me they form a single thing.' In the end or in the ending? Buñuel's phrase, '*al final*', could mean either, but in context seems to mean the first. The second is easier to accept and apply, though, and is confirmed by a later remark in the same interview (with de la Colina and Turrent). Asked about the two endings of the film – Pierre is crippled and mute, possibly dead, Pierre is hale and smiling, inquiring what Séverine is thinking about, just as he does near the beginning of the story – Buñuel said quite emphatically:

> There aren't two endings, only one ambiguous ending. I don't understand it. This indicates a lack of certainty on my part. It's the moment where I don't know what to do, I have various solutions, and don't decide on any of them. So in the ending I put my own uncertainty into the film. It's happened to me before.

We don't have to take him entirely literally, and probably shouldn't. But the sense of ambiguity is unambiguous, and perfectly matches what we see on the screen. This is not true if we take the previous remark I quoted in its apparently primary meaning.

The real and the imaginary don't form a single thing in Buñuel's *Belle de Jour*. Even if we choose to see Séverine's daydreams as more real than her respectable 'real' life, we are still making a distinction. And even if we choose to see all the events within the film as one long fantasy of Séverine's, we still need to imagine a real Séverine doing the fantasising, and to register the transitions within the fantasy when Séverine manifestly goes from one order of reality to another – stops dreaming or remembering, for instance, or shares a fantasy with Pierre. Perhaps Buñuel means that although the real and the imaginary are different within the film we can't always tell the difference – or he can't always tell the difference? A note in the screenplay suggests something like this. Séverine's story is

> interrupted a number of times by sequences which may be childhood memories, and above all waking dreams, in which characteristic obsessions appear and reappear.
>
> These sequences which, in principle, are imaginary, are not distinguished in any way, either in the image or the sound, from those which surround them, and which seem to describe objectively the relationships of the main characters and the development of these relationships.

The film is certainly faithful to this idea in its broadest, simplest sense. Séverine's memories and daydreams don't have special lighting or sound effects, the imaginary coachmen are manifestly as substantial as the real doctors, the main characters look and talk the same in both sets of sequences. This is a notion taken much further in *The Discreet Charm of the Bourgeoisie*, where we don't know characters are dreaming until we see them wake up, and in one case we are wrong even then, since the character who wakes is himself a figment of someone else's dream. Buñuel wants to insist on the permeability of the worlds of reality and dream, and on their equal status as objects of interest and aspects of lived life. He is also suggesting, in practice, that film is the perfect medium for this perception, since unless a director makes strenuous efforts to signal otherwise – through funny focus or strange angles, slow motion, sleepy music, etc. – we are disposed to believe everything we see on the screen is real. It is all real, Buñuel is saying. Why would the contents of our minds be less real than the contents of our living rooms?

But equal status is not the same as confusion. As Antonio Monegal very well says, 'the final transgression of the limits' between the real and the imaginary 'is based not on their indistinguishability but on their equivalence'. With two significant exceptions we know quite clearly when Séverine is living in clock time and when she is living in memory or fantasy, and it may help to describe these sequences and say why we know what they are.

Maurice Drouzy offers a helpful list. He says the film contains two flashbacks or memories, and five dreams or daydreams. They are 'easy to detect', he says. 'In each case (except the first) Séverine is in bed or visibly lost in thought. Once the scene is finished we return to the same situation as before. So there is no possible doubt about these sequences.' Raymond Durgnat similarly says 'fantasies are clearly signalled, either by their intrinsic improbabilities, or by the jingling of carriage bells'. But let's look.

1. The first sequence we have already considered and seen how it ends. Séverine is awake but rather abstracted, and Pierre's question and her answer suggest clearly that what we have been seeing is the material of her thoughts. We might want to say, with Paul Sandro, that we not only know where we are but that reality itself is defined as Pierre's place, since 'what began as Séverine's reality has now been reframed as her dream from Pierre's dominant perspective'. This formulation has the advantage of getting us to think not about the bottomless question of what is real and what is not, but about how the movie asks us to separate and order its different realities. For Séverine and for us, waking life with Pierre is real, and the landau is a supposedly harmless fantasy.

2. Having heard from a friend about Henriette's working in a brothel – 'But do they still exist, those places?' she asks, with a horribly failed attempt at casualness – Séverine is rattled and preoccupied when she gets home. She drops a vase full of flowers in the dining room, and knocks over a bottle of perfume in the bathroom. She says 'But what's the matter with me today?', and a woman in voice-over says 'Séverine, come quickly.' We see the legs of a little girl in close-up. 'Shiny black shoes, white socks', as the screenplay says, and as we can confirm. A man in overalls is kneeling beside her, and

'But what's the matter with me today?'

the camera moves up to reveal the rest of him and the little girl we take to be Séverine. He caresses her and kisses her. She closes her eyes. The same unseen woman's voice says 'Well, Séverine, are you coming or not?' Now we are in Pierre's study. He gets up to look for a book. Séverine, in a pink dressing gown, is sitting sewing. It is hard to read this little insert as anything other than a memory, although of course it could be a false memory, or the fantasy of a memory. What we are to do with this memory is another question. It certainly doesn't have the explanatory, exculpatory force of Kessel's prologue, which is its source.

3. I would add here a brief moment of memory which is not on Drouzy's list, but unmistakably places us in Séverine's mind. The thought is only a moment or so old, which is why it doesn't immediately seem like a memory. Séverine exchanges a few words with a woman at her tennis club, someone we have not seen before. No sooner has the woman left the screen than the voice of Henri Husson says 'Ah, the mysterious Henriette', adding 'The woman with two faces … the double life …'. Husson comes into view, and he and Séverine have a brief conversation about brothels. He rather insistently gives her the address of one, and tries to kiss her. Séverine asks him if he's mad. After Husson leaves the frame, the camera stays on Séverine's face, and we hear his voice on the soundtrack, as if inside her head. It is repeating the address he gave her: 'Madame Anaïs, 11 Cité Jean de Saumur'. The next shot is of a Paris street corner, with its blue sign indicating where we are: Cité Jean de Saumur. This is not just an extremely economical bit of narrative, getting us, in a series of deft moves, from the thought of Henriette to the actual person and from there to Séverine's new life. It also makes Husson a key player in Séverine's decisions, not just an informant but a voice in her head – this is important for later developments in the film. And when the street sign echoes that voice, we not only elide all the stages of Séverine's thought which got her from knowing where to go to actually going there, we seem to see her thought itself come alive, as if, with Husson's aid, she had conjured up the street by magic, made it appear in her reality as it appears on our screen. A picture, in other words, of a mind in the act of remembering but also concretely making a future, exchanging its old fantasies for their real-life equivalent in otherwise Pierre-dominated time.

4. After some hesitations, on the street and in a park, Séverine, wearing dark glasses, mounts the stairs of Mme Anaïs's building. As she climbs, we hear Latin being chanted in voice-over. We see a priest offering the host to a girl – the girl we saw being caressed by the workman – dressed as for a first communion. She keeps her mouth closed, refuses the host. The priest continues in Latin, then says 'Séverine, Séverine, what's the matter with you?' The girl closes her eyes. We are back with Séverine on the staircase, now

'Séverine, what's the matter with you?'

outside Mme Anaïs's apartment. Again, it's hard to see this insert as anything other than a memory of some sort; and hard not to connect it to the previous flashback. The child Séverine is refusing the host because of the workman's caresses – because, we assume, of her sense, justified or not, of her own complicity in those caresses. The effect of the two inserts taken together is not to provide an explanation for Séverine's behaviour but to suggest that at least it has a history, and that she, at any rate, is connecting her present temptations with a molestation in the past.

5. After her first day's work at the brothel, Séverine takes a shower and burns her underwear. Hearing the sounds of Pierre's return home, she rushes to get into her bed, pulls up the covers and pretends to have been asleep. She says she doesn't feel well, can't go out to dinner as planned. Pierre says fine. The camera moves in on Séverine, her eyes open, then close again, and we hear cow-bells in the soundtrack. A herd of wild bulls rushes past. We see a huge pot boiling over an open fire. Husson's voice asks if the soup is ready, and Pierre, on screen, but without moving his lips, says it's frozen,

Bulls and soup

and he can't warm it up. Soup is a feminine noun in French, so he is literally saying she is frozen, and he can't warm her up. The symbolism is so flagrant that it feels like a trap or a joke. This feeling is exacerbated when Pierre asks if the bulls have names, and Husson says most of them are called Remorse, except for the one called Expiation. Husson takes his hat off and bows his head, stands with Pierre in silence, and the composition of the shot presents a recognisable and very funny parody of Millet's painting *The Angelus*. Over a view of Husson's and Pierre's legs and feet, Husson asks what time it is, and Pierre says it's 'between two and five. Not later than five.' These are the hours Séverine has told Mme Anaïs she is free, and which have warranted her the name of Belle de Jour. Husson asks Pierre how his wife is, and Pierre asks Husson if he'd like to say hello. We see Séverine, wearing a white dress, tied to a pole. Husson insults her violently in words and also throws handfuls of mud at her. Pierre stands by, arms crossed. Séverine, whose lips don't move either, begs Pierre to stop, and tells him she loves him. Then we are back at Mme Anaïs's apartment. Séverine has returned, but is greeted harshly, because she has been away for a week. 'I don't want amateurs working here,' Anaïs says. 'There's the street for that.' This insert makes sense only as an image of Séverine's guilt, what she is thinking as she lies in bed, perhaps what she is dreaming when she falls asleep. It also signals the passage of time, as when it ends seven days have gone by since we last saw Séverine in the present moment. The trouble is that the sequence makes far too much symbolic sense, and is so elaborately and tritely orchestrated, so full of tacky images of piety, that it suggests both that Séverine is enjoying her guilt, perhaps finding in it a secondary source of pleasure, and that Buñuel is up to something. But what?

6. Husson calls on Séverine, but she tells the maid to tell him she's not in. Husson hears the whole exchange, and leaves. Séverine puts down the magazine she was reading, and looks thoughtful. Séverine and Husson are now sitting in a bar, which is the same as the place where they met at the beginning of the movie – a ski resort, and they are wearing the same sweaters and slacks as before. We see their faces in profile, facing each other, in tight close-up. He says he wants to write her a letter, and she welcomes the idea eagerly. Her manner is enormously friendly, collaborative. He says he needs to give her a receipt, and breaking a bottle on the table, asks if this will do. Séverine smiles and says yes, and they both disappear beneath the table. Pierre and Séverine's friend Renée, now revealed to be sitting at the same table, seem undisturbed, and Pierre asks calmly what they are doing. Renée peers under the table, and says 'Oh, nothing. They're having a good time.' She invites Pierre to look himself but he says he'd rather she told him about it. The table starts to rock backwards and forwards, and Renée says Husson has taken out a small envelope, and that it contains lily seeds. Pierre is now a little troubled, and lights a cigarette. 'I see,' he says. The next shot shows a Paris street, the Champs-Elysées as it happens, and a character we have not seen before buys a copy of the *Herald Tribune*. This is perhaps the strangest of the fantasy sequences in the film, clearly signalled as imaginary by Séverine's thoughtful look as she puts the magazine down, and by its unlikely content, impossible in terms of the

relations among the characters as we know them. But the dream seems a good deal more disguised, less allegorical than the previous one, and certain details – the lilies, and the rocking movement of the table – are borrowed from Séverine's encounter with the necrophiliac Duke, an episode whose reality status is already dubious. It's clear that Séverine is acknowledging, in fantasy, a complicity with Husson which she denies in real life, that disappearing under the table with him is only apparently in contradiction with refusing to see him. But what is the nature of this complicity? It can't be just that he gave her the address of Mme Anaïs. And this sequence ends, very curiously, not with a later moment in Séverine's life but a moment in the life of someone she has not yet met, the Spanish gangster Hippolyte. We dive into one river, so to speak, and surface in another.

7. Husson shows up at the brothel. Séverine begs him to say nothing to Pierre, and says 'It all happens in spite of myself, I can't help it, I can't resist it. I know that one day I shall have to pay for what I've done.' 'Expiate' is what she literally says, as if she was remembering the name of one of her dream bulls. Husson says he doesn't feel like having sex with her, and leaves her some money. 'It's not for you,' he says, 'but you can buy some chocolates for Pierre, from me.' There is a close-up on Séverine and we hear the door close. We are now in a wooded landscape, identified in the screenplay as the Bois de Boulogne. Four top-hatted gents in black, one of them Pierre, back in the *fin de siècle* we already know, get down from a landau, and greet another group, among them

Old friends: Mme Anaïs greets Husson at the brothel

Husson. They set up for a duel. Both men fire, and the camera
reveals Séverine, tied to a tree, wounded in the temple, like Pierre
in Kessel's novel. Pierre kisses her, touches her wound with his
hand, looks at the blood. She's not dead, her eyes are open, and
they move, the rush and fall of the sea is heard in the soundtrack: a
memory of her excursion with Pierre away from Paris, when she
realised how much she loved him, and how that love wasn't
enough. And when she failed to tell him anything of what she was
thinking – we heard it in the soundtrack, but her lips didn't move,
as if this piece of unmistakable 'reality' was also a dream. Then we
return to Anaïs's apartment, where Séverine tells Anaïs she has to
leave, and won't come back. The time-frame is clear here, because
Anaïs asks if Husson has left. The meaning of this fantasy seems
obvious. Séverine is afraid Husson will tell Pierre about her
afternoons, and pictures herself as the victim of the pair of them.
But then the date and the décor are odd for such an elementary
worry. She is still in the old soft-porn novel – not the one by Kessel
but the one Séverine uses as the instrument of her fantasies. Could
it be that even exposure would be a decadent treat, whatever
Séverine's conscious rational fears are? Or has Séverine retreated
to her period piece out of shock? And again, what is Buñuel up to?

8.   Right at the end of the film, after the flurry of ambiguous
alternatives, Pierre and Séverine, in their apartment, talk of taking
a holiday, going to the mountains. The bells of the horse-harness
are very loud in the soundtrack, and it seems that both characters
can hear them, since Séverine invites Pierre to listen: '*Tu entends?*'
Séverine steps out on to the balcony of the apartment, and looks
down not on to the street where they live but the park we saw at the
beginning of the movie. She herself seems to be standing
somewhere else, since she has trees behind her, and not the façade
of a building. The landau approaches again, with the same two
horses and the same coachman and companion. As the carriage
passes below us, though, we see that it is empty. The carriage leaves
the frame, and the camera remains on the fallen leaves littering the
ground. The bells get louder, and the word 'FIN' appears on the
screen, then disappears. I need to defer a full consideration of this
sequence until we look at the whole puzzling finale of the film. This
is one of the two exceptions I mentioned to our knowing quite

clearly when Séverine is living in clock time and when she is living in memory or fantasy.

We can see at once that although Drouzy and Durgnat are not quite right about the details – we don't always return to the place where we started, there aren't always intrinsic improbabilities or jingling bells – they are on to something important. In *Belle de Jour* what is pictured as imaginary and what is pictured as real may both be questionable, as all fictional images are, but the narrative requires us to think about their difference. There is an immediate consequence of this insight. If the landau is imaginary and Séverine's apartment, say, is real, the brothel manifestly belongs to the same world as the apartment. We can't take it as an insert because on the movie's own terms it isn't signalled as such in any way, and even Buñuel is not going to have a character burning her actual bra and panties because she had a dream in them.

In the interview with de la Colina and Turrent, Buñuel amusingly gets himself into and out of trouble on this score. Having said that as far as he is concerned the imaginary and the real form a single thing, he reacts violently to the suggestion that Séverine's visits to the brothel could belong to her imaginary life. No, Buñuel says categorically. She has a 'normal life' and she has 'indecent' fantasies. We see the fantasies, but the brothel is not one of them, 'she really goes to the brothel. … Everything follows logically, it is real.' Then he backs off and resumes his usual stance on such issues: viewers are entitled to their opinions, they are right if they think they are, he is even willing to believe that their vision of the film is better than his. What we have just seen is a little flicker of film theory, ill-focused, and gone almost before it was there. Buñuel is saying both that interpretation is up to the viewer and that certain basic stylistic or narrative moves in his film ought to be seen as prior to interpretation – the way the letters of the alphabet, or the bare plot-line of a film or play or novel, although the product of interpretation themselves, in the sense of reading or hearing or seeing, are logically prior to what we usually call interpretation. If we can't get the letters to form the word *vertigo*, we can't talk about what caused it, and what its metaphorical implications are. If we don't agree that Othello has killed Desdemona, we can't argue about why he did it. In this instance, we don't have to accept Buñuel's version of things if we don't want to, but we do have to wonder why we would wish to refuse the sight of the gradual invasion of reality by fantasy, the thorough materialisation of Séverine's daydream, which can only occur if we see the brothel as real.

Of course we need to remember that *Belle de Jour* is a film, that we have only images of reality at best. But we have only images of the imaginary too, and the difference between the two worlds is not given to us as a basic fact but offered to us as the product of a whole series of signs laid out for our construal. Buñuel would say the world outside the film is like this too, except when some particularly stubborn bit of material reality gets up and hits you in the face. He would also say, in his militant Surrealist mode, that we need to remake the real world in the light of the imaginary. 'The cinema', he suggested in a lecture reprinted in the recent book *An Unspeakable Betrayal*, 'is the best instrument through which to express the world of dreams, of emotions, of instinct.' But this view requires us to imagine something better than the historical world we've got, and we do have other imaginings. Buñuel added that he did not 'favour a cinema exclusively devoted to the expression of the fantastic and the mysterious', and the ironic commentary scattered all over his late films reminds us that the imaginary forgets the real at its peril. In *The Phantom of Liberty*, a whole society of parents, teachers and policemen continues to search for a little girl who is standing in front of them – because she has been reported missing. They can't see the child because their minds are occupied by the force of the word. Buñuel was always interested in the considerable resistance and weird compliance which historical reality offers to the demands of dream – *The Criminal Life of Archibaldo de la Cruz* is built on this alternation, and *El* tests it to the limit – but in *Belle de Jour* he found his most elegant formula so far for such collisions and elisions.

The other exception to our knowing when Séverine is living in clock time and when she is living in memory or fantasy involves the curious sequence with the Duke, and Buñuel's comment here is distinctly riddling. He insists that Séverine's encounter with the Duke is also, within the fiction of the film, entirely real, 'it is not a dream or a daydream'. This proposition doesn't initially seem to pose a problem. Séverine, having worked in the brothel for some time, having encountered the large Asian who gives her the kind of pleasure her counterpart in the novel found with the porter from Les Halles, does a little freelance work in the Bois de Boulogne. The Duke picks her up at an open-air cafe, invites her to his château for what he calls '*une cérémonie religieuse, en quelque sorte*' ('a religious ceremony, as it were'). The

The Duke explains he is man of another age

En route to the ceremony

ceremony involves, as we have seen, masturbation and imaginary necrophilia, and the Duke, now wearing a monocle for additional old-time effect, approaches the coffin carrying a camera on a tripod and a bunch of lilies. He doesn't use the camera, and is angry when his butler asks if he should let the cats in – but why would the butler ask his question if the cats were not sometimes part of the ceremony? Buñuel removed from this scene, on the recommendation of his producers, a black mass set against the background of a reproduction of the Grünewald crucifixion, 'the most terrible image of Christ', Buñuel said, a painting of 'ferocious realism'. This is not your ordinary afternoon in the country, but it seems reasonable to treat the sequence as an analogue to the brothel in another register: the peculiarities here, if that is what they are, belong to the Duke, not Séverine's imagination. But then how did Séverine's landau, complete with identical coachmen, get into the Duke's possession, and haven't those cats slipped out of Séverine's initial fantasy into this encounter? Maybe they stowed away in the landau. On film, the returning faces of the coachmen are particularly striking. After all, we saw one of these men about to rape Séverine, on Pierre's instructions. We are not likely to forget him, and outside of films and fantasies, we don't know of any world where the creatures of dreams get good solid jobs in daylight working time.

It's tempting to construct an alternative sequence. Perhaps the scene with the Duke, although placed at the centre of the film, actually occurred earlier in story time, and is the source of Séverine's current fantasies. Where would this get us, though, and if she were already cruising the Bois de Boulogne why would she need to learn about Henriette and Mme Anaïs? So perhaps Buñuel is wrong, and we have to take the Duke as a fantasy, an elaborate development of the theme of the landau and the coachmen. Or we take the sequence as a reminder that a movie is a movie, and that narrative continuity is the virtue of small minds and can't be expected of an unrepentant Surrealist. Or Buñuel, on film as distinct from in his interviews, is suggesting that although the imaginary and the real can usually be separated, in *Belle de Jour* as in life, the separation is not always easy or even possible, and this sequence is there to remind us of uncertainty, to create a crossover, twilight territory of doubt.

We can take our pick here, but I would offer one further possibility. In the sequence with the Duke and everywhere in the film, Buñuel is concerned, discreetly and not so discreetly, to wreck the very idea of psychology. He accepts, let's say, the distinction between the mind and the world, but not the coherence or independence of the mind. The very idea of a personality, for Buñuel, is not only a construct but a repressive social fantasy. This is Buñuel's starkest departure from Kessel's novel – not in the plotting or the characters, but in his assumptions about the self and its consistency. Kessel is a talented psychological novelist working in a recognisable and very distinguished tradition – which includes Mme de la Fayette and Benjamin Constant, to say nothing of Stendhal and Proust. Even Proust, that great destroyer of psychological comfort, allows memory, at the end of his vast novel, to pull the self together over time. Psychology, in this context, is the collusion of reason and behaviour, a heroic exercise in understanding which is also a denial of much that escapes understanding. When Freud says there are no accidents in the unconscious, he is working purely in this vein. When he gives us, in his examples if not in his theory, every reason to believe the unconscious is one of the favourite playgrounds of accident, he is moving (unconsciously) closer to Buñuel.

The cats, the landau and the coachmen can't be confined to Séverine's daydream for the same reason that we will always wonder why the professor in the brothel, otherwise an entirely predictable comic instance of the taste for humiliation, needs an inkwell for his perversion, or what the Asian has in his little humming box, and why it turns the other women off but not Séverine. There is, in Buñuel's film world, no secure, explicable self in which these images and objects can be grounded. Séverine's memories, and her guilt, are real enough, part of the confusing litter of her mind, but they don't focus or create a personality. For Kessel, Séverine is not a case but a character, someone for whom he can feel love or affection. For Buñuel, she is neither a case nor a character, but a complicated plight, whose compulsions can't explain her because they erratically defeat the very idea of explanation, and because he keeps underlining their divergence. She is overcome by her sexual appetites, she freely indulges them. She hates deceiving Pierre, she loves her secret life. Marcel is the perfect opposite of Pierre, and also a version of Pierre found in the brothel, a Pierre with scars and gold teeth. The overwrought symbolism of her dreams, the Angelus, the flung mud, the duel, the obsessive presence of Husson in her mind and her life, the impossibility of linking her fantasies with any account of them she might give to her husband, all add up not to a person but to a kind of theatre, a human space where shreds of what once was psychology appear and disappear like broken dreams of organised knowledge.

5

··························

SÉVERINE AND THE WHEELCHAIR

The ending of *Belle de Jour* is where Buñuel most drastically rewrites Kessel – as distinct from adding to his story or departing from his assumptions. In both versions Marcel discovers Séverine's address, and Husson shows up at the brothel. But in the film Séverine does not conspire with Marcel to kill Husson. She doesn't conspire with anyone. Marcel appears one day in her apartment, looks at a photograph of Pierre, says he is beginning to understand her, and leaves, flinging the photograph and its frame on to the piano, saying, '*Voilà l'obstacle*' ('There is the obstacle'). In what appears to be a direct sequence of events, Marcel tells his pal Hippolyte to leave him the car, puts a revolver on the seat beside him, and sits and waits; Séverine in her apartment hears three shots, goes to the window, sees both Marcel's car driving off and a figure lying crumpled on the pavement; Marcel crashes into a car pulling out of the place where it is parked, gets out of his own car, panics and runs when he sees a policeman, decides to shoot it out and is killed. In a scene at a hospital, we learn that Marcel's victim was Pierre, who is still in a coma.

Time passes, signalled by different, rainy weather, and a shot of wind-blown autumn leaves superimposed on the façade of the building which contains Séverine's apartment. Indoors, Séverine is preparing a sweetened lemon drink for someone in a wheelchair – we see only the base of the chair and the person's legs. Séverine makes small talk, and we

'*Voilà l'obstacle*'

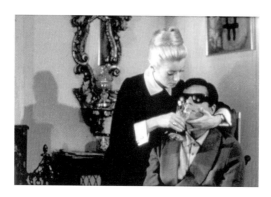

'You're getting better, you
know'

now see Pierre, in the wheelchair, totally paralysed, wearing dark glasses
and a dressing gown. He doesn't respond in any way to Séverine's
remarks. ('Everyone asks how you are. You're getting better, you know.
The Professor is very optimistic'). She tells him that since his accident she
no longer has her dreams. She lifts his chin, gives him a spoonful of
medicine. Still no sign of life.

The maid announces that Husson has come to call, and wants to see
Pierre. Séverine steps into another room to meet him. She asks him what
he wants to say to Pierre, and he says, gaily, 'Everything I know about
you.' Séverine is stunned. Husson explains that Pierre must be ashamed
of his dependence on her, and that knowledge of her exploits will no
doubt hurt him but probably help him – in other words, pretty much what
Séverine herself finally thinks in Kessel's novel. 'After that,' Husson adds
in a wonderful mixture of delicate sadism and acute moral insight, 'who
will be able to say that I am a cruel person?' He is a cruel person, but he
has found what may well be an altruistic use for his cruelty. He asks
Séverine if she wants to be present at the conversation. She doesn't reply,
he goes into the drawing room to see Pierre, closing the door behind him.

There follows the most haunting scene in the film, and one of the
most inward and sustained pieces of movie-making anywhere in Buñuel.
We simply watch Séverine waiting. We see a sofa, which she briefly sits,
almost lies, on, her hands making a gesture just short of what we would
call wringing. She gets up and leaves the room. Her legs and feet come
towards us in close-up, the camera lifts to follow her hand as it runs jerkily
along the edge of a marble-topped table. Then we see her face and torso
in stark profile against a glass door. Expressionless. A clock, somewhere

in the apartment, strikes five. We see Husson leaving; no one shows him out. When she first thought of Husson telling Pierre about her afternoon activities, Séverine imagined a duel out of a *fin de siècle* novel, and included her own beautifully suffering self. Now, as Husson presumably gives Pierre the details, we don't know what she sees, and we supply all the shades of possibility, from despair to some sort of ultimate relief. We supply the shades not only because there is nothing of this sort for us to see, only a pale young woman in an apartment, but because Séverine, although she looks anxious enough, doesn't appear to be feeling half of what we think she ought to feel. Buñuel, having filled our imagination with fictions, leaves us alone with our gaudy projections, and the sheer sobriety of what's left on the screen is startling.

Husson leaves, and Séverine goes in to see Pierre. Here also Bunuel introduces a remarkable shot, a visual version of controlled anxiety. The camera picks up Séverine in the doorway to the left, a troubled look on her face. She crosses the room along the front of the frame, so that we see Pierre at the back, slightly out of focus, and then lose him. Her movement is not absolutely straight, she goes all the way around Pierre at some distance, looking at him all the time. It's as if she has to circle him before she can talk to him. From the far right of the picture, but closer to him now, she whispers his name. The camera tracks slowly across to show him still motionless. A tear now stains his face. Séverine sits down, takes up her sewing, falls back in her seat, pensive. No movement from Pierre. A close-up shows his inert hands, the right one palm up, lying on his knees. Is there a faint flicker or twitch of the hands here? Many viewers have seen one, and interpreted it as the sign of Pierre's death – killed, presumably, by Husson's news. There is no twitch, but the close-up is sudden, and taken from a strange highish angle, which makes Pierre's hands look more than merely useless. It is followed by an extremely low-angle shot looking up at Pierre's unmoving face and blank glasses. Now there's a view of Séverine's face, which shows a movement of surprise. Has she realised that Pierre is dead? No, because she is smiling. We hear the cow-bells of her dream about remorse and expiation. Pierre too is smiling. He has taken off his dark glasses, and asks, 'What are you thinking about, Séverine?' She says she was thinking of him, he gets up, pours himself a drink, and a mewing of cats joins the sound of the bells on the soundtrack. Pierre and Séverine start the conversation about their holidays which we have already looked at.

Pierre's paralysis

Now one of the joys of cinema is that anything can happen between shots – centuries could pass, for example. We could, if we wished, read every blatant breach of narrative continuity as an ellipsis. If a person is wearing different clothes in a shot which seems to follow directly from the previous one, she may have had time to change between frames – may fictionally have had time, that is, as she manifestly had time outside the fiction. I don't think this quite explains why Séverine shows up at the Duke's château wearing her natty leather coat with fur trimmings, and leaves putting on her glossy black raincoat. No doubt we don't always wish to avail ourselves of the opportunity to play with imagined clocks and calendars, and movie-makers employ devoted professional people to ensure we don't get the opportunity too often.

But there is no reason why we should not read the closing sequence of *Belle de Jour* quite literally if we want to. We can't, in such a scheme, have a Pierre who dies and then gets up and pours himself a drink, but we can have everything else. Marcel shoots him, he is paralysed, Husson informs on Séverine, Pierre is distraught, time passes – while Séverine is sewing, for instance, or between one visible moment of sewing and another, and Pierre gets better. Husson was right, the bad news was good for him in the long run. The problem with this interpretation is not its implausibility, but the reverse. It is perfectly plausible, and perfectly banal, and requires us to believe that Buñuel, whatever he said about his ambiguous conclusion, replaced Kessel's grim and moralising pessimism with the irenic suggestion that everything will be all right in the end. It is important that this more or less straight and boring interpretation is possible, though, because it shadows all other interpretations, makes them look reprehensibly nifty or oblique, and because it returns us to one of the basic facts of film: everything we see is true in one sense, since we have just been an eye-witness of it.

The most dramatic claim to make about Buñuel's ending would be that Pierre both does and doesn't die. This would have to be seen as two endings rather than a single ambiguous one, but we can ignore the director's views if we have to. With Pierre's death, Séverine would be punished for her immoralities, and punished more extremely, if less insidiously, than in Kessel; with his continuing life, she would have cleared up her psyche and their marriage, come through her multiple ordeal and out the other side into happiness. The two endings refute each other: the first points to the irresponsibility of the second, the second accuses the first of vindictive conventionality. We can't put them together or give either of them up. They stare at each other like a model of perpetual deconstruction.

I think this is close to the feeling the film leaves us with, but I don't think it works quite this way. Most viewers, attuned to the alternations between the real and the imaginary in Séverine's life, feel the story has forked into fantasy before we get to the apparent contradictions of this final scene. Somewhere, we left the given reality behind, the place Séverine repeatedly wakes up to and goes home to, Pierre's world. But where? A good candidate is the scene where Séverine hears the shots Marcel presumably fires at Pierre. We hear them before she does, or before we know she does, over a view of an apparently empty apartment. Then Séverine, who has been hidden by the back of the sofa, sits up into the frame. Has she been asleep? Has she dreamed the shots? Is she dreaming now? Perhaps everything that follows is a long guilty fantasy, a more realistic version of the duel daydream, and one in which Pierre gets shot instead of her. Even Husson's arrival would be the projection of Séverine's compunction. Two fairly appealing inferences would then present themselves. The incoherence of the film's ending is a reflection of Séverine's uncertain mind. We have not left the dream, and the dream plays out the two extreme alternatives, Pierre's death and resurrection, Séverine's doom and deliverance. Or the bad dream ends just before Pierre stands up and pours himself a drink. He wasn't paralysed at all except in Séverine's fantasy. Why is he wearing the dressing gown and dark glasses that he wore in the dream? Don't be difficult. Perhaps he's only got one dressing gown.

The trouble with these interpretations is not that we can't (more or less) get them to work, but that they are too tempting and seem desperately wrongheaded, whatever their logical or narrative attractions. More precisely, we can abandon any of these interpretations easily enough, but it's amazingly hard to give up the game of interpretation itself, the attempt to make the events of this movie behave like the events of a proper story, however complicated. It's a false trail, but we stay on it, as if addicted; of course we are supposed to stay on it, even as we lose all faith in its destination, because the trail and its disappointments are the very movement of our watching the movie. Why is it a false trail? How do we know it is? Well, we don't know for sure, but the pleasure of the movie seems different from its riddles, larger, simpler, more direct. The riddles are part of the pleasure, certainly, but far from all of it; they are absorbed into a more capacious sense of having seen something, having witnessed a torment which was also a liberation, a liberation which seems sadly restricted. This is what is played out in our efforts to rationalise the narrative, to find the last fork into fantasy. Like Séverine, we need the double story and try to refuse it; try to sustain it and watch it collapse. Our attempts at resolution fail, but that failure, if we work at it enough, becomes the form our success takes.

There are two images in the movie for this state of affairs, what we might think of as scenes of instruction, although the term is a little heavy for these glancing moments. One occurs right at the end, and is extraordinarily graceful, quiet and complex. We have previously examined it. Séverine's landau passes beneath her window, or across the park her mind has moved her to. There is no mistaking the sense of relief conveyed by the fact that the carriage is empty. This is a happy ending, a form of exorcism, and far more convincing than Séverine's assertion to the motionless Pierre that she doesn't dream any more. The very presence of the landau in this scene, and of the bells and the cats in the soundtrack, prove that claim to be quite wrong. More important is what she dreams. There is no prickly if affectionate couple in the landau as there was at the beginning, no masochistic heroine on the way to insult and violation. The story is not going to start again, even if the disappearance of the word 'FIN' before the film's end creates an eerie effect of incompletion. But the happy ending is still only imagined, as far we can see. Séverine needs to return to the landscape of her dream in order to experience it. We can of course see the empty landau as the promise of a happy sex life with Pierre in the unfantasised Paris bedroom, but that seems rather bluntly hopeful, and doesn't match the pardoned

The end: an image about to disappear

but tamed mood of the film's last images. We end as we started, not with Séverine's waking, but sharing her dream. She now has a quieter alternative to life, but it's still an alternative, still not living. Only an old novel, or the final frames of a movie.

The other image is far from graceful or quiet. It is so crass that it looks like, and must in part be, one of Buñuel's jokes about the very idea of intelligible meaning. There are similar moments in *Viridiana* and in *That Obscure Object of Desire*, where Buñuel resorts to comic, crashingly obvious allegories which merely duplicate, in visual terms, what we know perfectly well already. In *Viridiana*, the heroine's plight is abruptly represented by the condition of a bee falling into a rainwater butt. In *That Obscure Object*, when Mathieu finally thinks he's set a functioning trap for the much desired Conchita, his servant appears with a patently rubber mouse he says he's just caught. It's not just that these images are transparent and unnecessary. They are also miles away from Buñuel's usual ways of telling stories and creating sense. So what is he doing? Partly, I think, he is resorting to Surrealist teasing: we are in the habit of looking very hard for meaning, and he is briefly and pointlessly going to make it absurdly easy for us. See if we like it. But partly he is also engaging in an elaborate double bluff: the obvious meaning can't be the one we want, but the film has momentarily frozen into symbol, and this must mean something. It could mean: Don't look for symbols, but there are better ways of telling us that, starting by doing without symbols, even parodied ones. It could also mean: Symbols are irresistible, even when (or because) they hit you over the head, but that doesn't guarantee they mean anything beyond what you already knew.

The image in question in *Belle de Jour* is that of Pierre's wheelchair. We have seen him sitting in it (seeming to die in it) and leaving it at the end, but he and we have also seen it earlier in the film. Séverine picks Pierre up at the hospital where he works; they are meeting for lunch. She seems relaxed and happy. He remarks on the change in her, and the pleasure he has in seeing her smile. She says, 'I do feel much better, it's true,' and we grin or groan at the irony he can't possibly get. Séverine's relation with Marcel is developing nicely, a perfect, pleasurable complement to her dutiful, ide-alised life with Pierre, an arrangement of body and mind which Marcel seems to understand, even if he doesn't care for it. She likes being with him but she loves Pierre. 'They are two very different things,' she says to Marcel in the scene which immediately precedes that of her meeting Pierre at the hospital. The whole scheme is about to collapse, though, since right after this sequence Husson shows up at the brothel. Séverine meets Pierre between a rendezvous with the man who now embodies her other world and an unexpected encounter with the man who will make her two worlds crumble into one.

Pierre, pushing his luck, and presumably referring indirectly to their improved sex life – nothing like successful away games to enhance the performance at home – says wistfully he'd like one day to hear her give him a great piece of news, '*une grande nouvelle*'. She doesn't understand what he's talking about until he explains. 'What I would like above all: a child.' Séverine doesn't answer. They leave the hospital, hand in hand, and we hear the siren of an ambulance in the soundtrack. Just a reality effect, of course, this is a hospital. But do we feel the same way about the empty wheelchair someone has left on the sidewalk? Pierre doesn't. He stops and stares; stares offscreen before we see what he sees. Then Pierre and the wheelchair are both in the frame. Séverine asks him what he's looking at. He says, 'Nothing. … It's this contraption [*cet*

Séverine and Pierre meet at the hospital

'It's this contraption …'

engin], it struck me. … I don't know why, it's strange.' Séverine says it's not strange at all, and he says she's right. Once Pierre has cast a last look at the wheelchair they get into their car, and the scene is over.

In the wake of the conversation about the child and what we know about Séverine's pleasure with Marcel, Pierre's fascination with the wheelchair seems like an obscure intuition of something he will never get his mind around consciously: not his childlessness, but his inability to reach Séverine, his paralysis in the midst of apparent movement, his unsuspected cuckoldry. The wheelchair is waiting for him, empty because only he is to occupy it. He knows this, but can't imagine why. Once we have seen the film through to the end, of course, we realise the wheelchair is waiting for him in an entirely different sense: not as a metaphor but as his literal fate, the chair he sits in during the final sequence, paralysed as the result of the activities, principally, of a person he doesn't even know. No wonder the police are said to be at a loss in this case.

'Buñuel is nothing if not fatalistic,' Andrew Sarris writes.

> Even the hapless husband is granted a mystical premonition when he sees an empty wheelchair in the street. It is destined for him, and the concreteness of Buñuel's visual imagery is so intense that we feel that the wheelchair is destined for Pierre as Pierre is destined for the wheelchair.

Everything is right here except the fatalism, very remote from Buñuel's vision at any stage. Marcel didn't have to shoot Pierre, and the shooting certainly didn't have to produce precisely the result it had. But why would Buñuel want to show us Pierre getting this glimpse of a future that seems the reverse of fated? The intense concreteness of the scene is inseparable from a sense of intrusive allegory. We don't need to see things flagged in this way, and Buñuel knows we don't. The hapless husband, surely, is looking at an image of destiny so crudely and literally put in his way, so thoroughly beyond his possible comprehension, that it mocks the very thought of destiny. And what is impossible for him is too easy for us. The film at this moment looks like a story anxious to give itself away, like a joke that has arrived at its punch-line too soon, and is already stumbling to get back on track.

Why would Buñuel do this, can there be any mileage in simulating ineptitude? None at all. The ineptitude, in a limited sense, is quite real. 'He leaves in miscalculations,' Pauline Kael says, 'and fragments that don't work – like the wheelchair on the sidewalk in *Belle de Jour*.' This is a fragment that couldn't work. Buñuel can't believe in the closure, or even the seriousness, of plot, and like a person achieving irony through overpoliteness, expresses his doubts in the form of excess. He is genuinely clumsy about his foreshadowed end, and makes it more or less impossible for us to see Pierre's plight, anticipated or lived, however interpreted, as anything other than a melodramatic and convenient fiction. Convenient for everyone except Pierre. He gets into and out of the wheelchair as much for our sake as for Séverine's. We (and / or she) place him there because we sternly feel someone has to pay for her escapades. Then we need him to walk again because we feel badly about our own ridiculous righteousness. 'I put my own uncertainty into the film,' Buñuel said. He did something more durable and substantial than that. He made a picture of uncertainty out of the certainties he showed us how to fail to reach.

6

. . . .

LATE BUÑUEL

'The movie comes close to serenity,' Pauline Kael wrote of *The Discreet Charm of the Bourgeoisie*, 'and it's a deep pleasure to see that the unregenerate anarchist-atheist has found his own path to grace.' She identified 'serenity' and 'enchantment' in *That Obscure Object of Desire*; and French critics were discovering serenity even earlier in Buñuel's work. Both Jean-Louis Comolli and Jean Collet, in *Cahiers du Cinéma* and *Figues du Temps* respectively, invoke the term in relation to *Belle de Jour*. In a documentary film, Buñuel's co-writer Jean-Claude Carrière talks of repairs and something that resembles repentance.

> It struck me very often that the first shot ever shot by Buñuel was a razor ... breaking an eye. His last shot was a woman's hand ... mending a slit ... in a piece of linen. As if he was at the end of his life repairing the wound he made at the beginning.

These are indeed, respectively, the opening image of *Un Chien andalou* and the closing image of *That Obscure Object of Desire*, but surely Carrière's conclusion is too conciliatory, and surely serenity is not the right word for the mood of these late films – say the six (relatively) glamorous colour films starting with *Belle de Jour*, and continuing with *The Milky Way*, *The Discreet Charm of the Bourgeoisie*, *The Phantom of Liberty* and *That Obscure Object of Desire*. I know that's only five films, but we need to make an exception for *Tristana*, which comes right in the middle of the series, and yet, as far as I know, has never looked to anyone like a candidate for serenity. Maybe the mood we're interested in came upon Buñuel only when he was shooting in France, and only when he was working with Carrière.

Linda Williams is right to be suspicious of the 'myth of Buñuel the mellowing Surrealist master', but the notions I have recalled can't simply be wrong. They are genuine attempts to describe an altered climate, a late moment, in Buñuel's career, and probably need to be refined rather than thrown out. Colour, France and Carrière certainly have a lot to do with this mood. After *Belle de Jour*, Buñuel never abandoned Eastmancolor, and his last three films were all shot by Edmond Richard. He had French actors who appeared in film after film – not the sort of dense repertory company that Bergman created but a set of recognisable faces, shapes and styles which are part of each film's signature, a kind of human landscape: Georges Marchal, Michel Piccoli and Pierre Clementi among the major roles, Muni, François Maistre and a number of others among the minor or passing parts. Carrière, who co-wrote *Belle de Jour*, *The Milky Way*, *The Discreet Charm of the Bourgeoisie*, *The Phantom of Liberty* and *That Obscure Object of Desire*, as well as *Diary of a Chambermaid*, finally brought out in Buñuel a lightness of touch he had often sought but not often achieved – a lightness missing from *Tristana*, which Buñuel wrote with Julio Alejandro, after a novel by Pérez Galdós, and which has quite other virtues. Carrière's other credits would confirm this view, if we needed confirmation: *Viva Maria*, *Cyrano de Bergerac* and *Milou en mai*, although he also wrote *Danton* and *The Return of Martin Guerre*. Buñuel himself said he moved towards 'tenderness' in his later work, although he added immediately, and characteristically, that 'one can be tender and cruel' at the same time.

There are many Buñuels, and it's useful to sort them out. There is an experimental silent Buñuel; a commercial Mexican Buñuel; a latish

Civilisation collapses in *The Exterminating Angel*

Spanish Buñuel; a later French Buñuel; and various unclassifiable fellows in between. *Viridiana* is a Spanish film, and feels Spanish; but *The Exterminating Angel*, made in Mexico, and *Diary of a Chambermaid*, made in France, feel pretty Spanish too, in spite of Carrière's work on the latter, and I think critics are right to see *Belle de Jour* as inaugurating a final series of French films: late Buñuel.

What does 'Spanish' mean here, and does it make sense to fling these national stereotypes around? Not much sense but some; as long as we are only clearing the ground, making working distinctions. 'Spanish' means austere and haunted in a way Buñuel's French films are not; further from whatever Pauline Kael means by grace. Look at Fernando Rey in *Viridiana* and *Tristana*; then look at him in *The Discreet Charm of the Bourgeoisie* and *That Obscure Object of Desire*. He is elegant and imposing in all four films, but also comic and exotic in the last two, out of his element – the element where he lives has disappeared. He is humiliated in all four films, but ridiculous only in the last two. In the first two films, where he ought to be ridiculous, as at many moments in *Tristana*, he is desolate and pathetic, a historical ruin. 'Spain' is the place where this man is at home, even in distress; 'France' is the place where his very distress is ludicrous.

But this is where we need to be careful, and remember that increased tenderness doesn't have to mean lessened cruelty. Buñuel's late lightness is a wonderful thing, and quite different from the bleak, dark humour of many of his films, *El*, for instance, or even *Los Olvidados*, which has a number of sinister gags among its Mexican miseries. But he hasn't repented, and he isn't repairing old damages. Could we want him to? Could he do it without betraying almost everything his career as a film-maker represented? What would it mean for him to find a path to grace, his own or anyone else's?

Buñuel used to say there was only one of his films he would like to remake: *The Exterminating Angel*, with classy English actors like Laurence Olivier and John Gielgud. That way, when things fall apart and the dinner guests become barbarians, something that looked like civilisation itself would be seen collapsing, rather than the merely stilted world of the Mexican middle classes, or worse, a not entirely convincing actorly impression of those classes. Buñuel was talking, of course, about the image of civilisation rather than the thing itself, and in a sense he did remake that film – several times. That's what his French films are, and what late Buñuel is: France is to the idea of society what Olivier and

Gielgud are to the idea of acting. In *Belle de Jour, The Discreet Charm of the Bourgeoisie, The Phantom of Liberty, That Obscure Object of Desire* and to a lesser extent, *The Milky Way*, society not only skates on thin ice, but mistakes the thinness of the ice for a sign of high culture. The discreetly charming bourgeoisie of all these films offers the perfect model for a civilisation which doesn't know how barbarous it is – the fluent fulfilment of Adorno's worst prophecies about late capitalism.

The glossy, fashion-conscious visual universe of these films, the stylish actors and comfortable restaurants, the easy access to bishops and ambassadors, distinguished doctors, the flock of servants and receptionists, the occasional terrorists and bombs, all suggest a modernity which is thoroughly pleased with itself, and capable of the firmest suppression of any sense of trouble. This is a world which is beyond satire, and the old disruptions of Surrealism are not going to make any mark on it, because ordinary life, in this place, is already as arbitrary and erratic as anything a Surrealist could dream up. So Buñuel takes us through the world, with his impeccable dead pan, and his characters, under the illusion of living well, indeed while actually living pretty well, play out the cosy decline of the West. We are not after all so far from the ghastly social occasions of *L'Age d'or*, and the sight of the Marquis de Sade staggering out of a château after murdering his last victim. Buñuel hasn't forgiven anyone. Only the laughter has changed; it stretches out, takes a walk, reflects the modified impatience of a man who has almost learned how to wait.

The bourgeoisie goes on

Not all of this is in *Belle de Jour*, and I have been speaking of Buñuel's late French films as if they made up a single domain. But it all starts in *Belle de Jour*: with the slight woodenness of Jean Sorel as Pierre, forerunner of several handsome men who mistake their easy habits for lived life; with the mannered performance of Pierre Clémenti, a portrait of the thug as tousled drop-out; with Catherine Deneuve's clothes and shoes, a whole exhibition of 60s smartness, that age which thought, among other things, that style was both surface and depth. An interesting chain of associations runs from Deneuve to the photographer David Bailey, whom she married, and who was the inspiration for the David Hemmings character in Antonioni's fashion-filled *Blow-Up*. Later, as everyone knows, Deneuve became the face of Chanel; reading backwards it looks as if Séverine found a whole vocation in her fabulous, passive fantasies rather than her afternoon work.

Belle de Jour also has the plush Paris apartment, '*style XVIe arrondissement*', as the screenplay says, a place where even dreams of punishment would have to have a certain elegance; and above all it has its brothel, that polite and friendly and underpopulated refuge, more like a

Style and serenity in the brothel

libertine convent than a house of ill fame, a quiet flat where the clients are only moderately weird and moderately vulgar, and the madame is cooler and classier than the French aristocrats in Proust. This is not a literal picture of society, adapted and glossified for the movies. It is a picture of an idea of society, husbands, marriage, clothes, wealth, comfort, vice, deviance, a kind of calendar illustration or stylised fiction. It corresponds in part to the images of life which contemporary advertising offered to movie viewers and magazine readers; but it turns that advertising into a travesty of a mode of thought.

If advertising imagined brothels at all, it would imagine them like this, discreetly comic or softly, shabbily romantic. Mme Anaïs tells Séverine that Monsieur Adolphe, her first client, is *'un homme très simple'*, meaning his sexual demands are quite straightforward. Soon after one of the other girls in the brothel says that working with the professor who likes to play at being humiliated is 'not complicated', and adds, 'If they were all like him … .' For a second we seem to glimpse the more difficult and no doubt more dangerous clients, the ones who are complicated and not straightforward, and when we later learn that Séverine is much in demand, we try to imagine her in bed with people quite different from the stylised figures we have seen. But we can't do it. There are no others. They can no more inhabit this brothel, or this movie, than we can live in the non-existent rooms behind the windows of a two-dimensional stage street.

In this respect the film itself begins to resemble Séverine's imaginings. They are grand and old-fashioned, involving a kind of historical fancy dress, as we saw earlier in this book. The film's vision of itself is rigorously up-to-date, and for that reason seem so perfectly to belong to its time: acting, dress, furnishing, polite idea of vice, everything. But both Séverine and the film hide the world behind an image of the world. We see only what they see or show; but we know it's not all there is. There is a serenity in *Belle de Jour* and in all of Buñuel's late films, but it is not his. It is the false and fragile serenity of the society he pictures. It is a confection of denial, and it can't last, Buñuel wants to suggest. Unless of course it lasts forever.

CREDITS

· ·

Belle de Jour/Bella di Giorno

France/Italy
1967

Production Companies
Robert and Raymond
Hakim present
Paris Film Productions
(Paris)/Five Film (Rome)
production
Production Manager
Henri Baum
Unit Manager
Marc Goldstaub
Production Administrator
Robert Demollière
Production Secretary
Jacqueline Delhomme
Director
Luis Buñuel
Assistant Director
Jacques Fraenkel
Assistant to the Director
Pierre Lary
Script Supervisor
Suzanne Durrenberger
Screenplay
Luis Buñuel,
Jean-Claude Carrière
Based on the novel by
Joseph Kessel
Director of Photography
Sacha Vierny
Camera Operator
Philippe Brun
Assistant Camera
Pierre Li, Lionel Legros
Stills Photography
Raymond Voinquel
Editor
Louisette Hautecoeur
Assistant Editor
Walter Spohr
Art Director
Robert Clavel
Assistant Art Director
Marc Robert Desages
Set Decorator
Maurice Barnathan

Properties
Pierre Roudeix
**Miss Deneuve's
Costumes by**
Yves Saint-Laurent
Costumer
Hélène Nourry
Make-up
Janine Jarreau
Hairstylist
Simone Knapp
Sound Engineer
René Longuet
Assistant Sound
Pierre Davoust

Cast
Catherine Deneuve
Séverine Serizy
Jean Sorel
Pierre Serizy
Michel Piccoli
Henri Husson
Geneviève Page
Madame Anaïs
Pierre Clémenti
Marcel
Françoise Fabian
Charlotte
Macha Méril
Renée
Muni
Pallas
Maria Latour
Mathilde
Claude Cerval
man
Michel Charrel
footman
Iska Khan
Asian client
Bernard Musson
majordomo
Marcel Charvey
Professor Henri
François Maistre
teacher

Francisco Rabal
Hippolyte
Georges Marchal
the duke
Francis Blanche
Monsieur Adolphe

[uncredited]
Bernard Fresson
Le Grele
Dominique Dandrieux
Catherine
Brigitte Parmentier
Séverine as a child
D. de Roseville
coachman
Pierre Marcay
intern
Adélaïde Blasquez
maid
Marc Eyraud
barman
Max Elloy
the duke's butler
Luis Buñuel
man in cafe

9,000 feet
100 minutes

Colour by
Eastmancolor

Credits compiled by
Markku Salmi,
BFI Filmographic Unit

BIBLIOGRAPHY

· ·

Aranda, Francisco, *Luis Buñuel*, trans. and
ed. D. Robinson (New York: Da Capo, 1976).

Aub, Max, *Conversaciones con Buñuel*
(Madrid: Aguilar, 1984).

Buache, Freddy, *The Cinema of Luis
Buñuel*, trans. Peter Graham (London: Tantivy
Press, 1973).

Buñuel, Luis, *Belle de Jour* (French) (Paris:
L'Avant-Scene du Cinéma, 1971).

———, *Belle de Jour* (English), trans.
Robert Adkinson (London: Lorrimer, 1971).

———, *Mon Dernier Soupir* (Paris: Robert
Laffont, 1982).

———, *My Last Sigh*, trans. A. Israel
(New York: Knopf, 1983).

———, *An Unspeakable Betrayal*, trans.
Garrett White (Berkeley, Los Angeles and
London: University of California Press, 2000).

de la Colina, José, and Tomás Pérez
Turrent, *Luis Buñuel: Prohibido Asomarse al
Interior* (Mexico City: Joaquin Mortiz, 1986).

Drouzy, Maurice, *Luis Buñuel: Architecte du
rêve* (Paris: Lherminier, 1978).

Durgnat, Raymond, *Luis Buñuel* (London:
Studio Vista, 1967).

Edwards, Gwynne, *The Discreet Art of Luis
Buñuel* (London: Marion Boyars, 1982).

Evans, Peter William, *The Films of Luis
Buñuel* (Oxford: Clarendon, 1995).

Fuentes, Carlos, 'The Discreet Charm of
Luis Buñuel', in Mellen (ed.), *The World of
Luis Buñuel*.

Higginbotham, Virginia, *Luis Buñuel*
(Boston: Twayne, 1979).

Kael, Pauline, 'Saintliness', in *Going Steady*
(Boston: Little, Brown, 1970).

———, 'Anarchist's Laughter', in *Reeling*
(Boston: Little, Brown, 1976).

———, 'Cutting Light', in *When the
Lights Go Down* (New York: Holt, Rhinehart
and Winston, 1980).

Kessel, Joseph, *Belle de Jour* (Paris:
Gallimard, 1928).

Mellen, Joan (ed.), *The World of Luis
Buñuel* (New York: Oxford University Press,
1978).

Monegal, Antonio, *Luis Buñuel de la
literatura al cine* (Barcelona: Anthropos, 1993).

Sandro, Paul, *Diversions of Pleasure: Luis
Buñuel and the Crises of Desire* (Columbus:
Ohio State University Press, 1987).

Sarris, Andrew, 'The Beauty of *Belle de
Jour*', in *Confessions of a Cultist* (New York:
Simon and Schuster, 1970). Reprinted in Mellen
(ed.), *The World of Luis Buñuel*.

Williams, Linda, *Figures of Desire: a Theory
and Analysis of Surrealist Film* (Berkeley, Los
Angeles, Oxford: University of California
Press, 1992).

BFI FILM

BFI FILM CLASSICS

ROME OPEN CITY
(ROMA CITTÀ APERTA)

·····························

David Forgacs

BFI FILM CLASSICS

BFI FILM

CLASSICS

THE MAGNIFICENT
AMBERSONS

····························

V. F. Perkins

ALSO PUBLISHED

If you would like further information about future BFI Film Classics or about other books on film, media and popular culture from BFI Publishing, please write to:

BFI Film Classics
BFI Publishing
21 Stephen Street
London W1P 2LN